C000196335

**Gaia Holmes** is a poet and t previously made a living as a bu an oral historian and a lollypo a Hawthornden Fellowship an and her poem 'Guests' won t poetry. She has had two full length poetry collections published by Comma Press: *Dr James Graham's Celestial Bed* (2006) and *Lifting the Piano with One Hand* (2013), as well as *Tales from the Tachograph*, a collaborative work with Winston Plowes (Calder Valley Poetry, 2017). Her poems have appeared in various anthologies including *Milestones, I Belong Here, The Book of Love and Loss* and *Seductive Harmonies*. She lives in Halifax.

*Praise for Gaia Holmes*

'Within *Where the Road Runs Out* there is a magnificent meditation on the spaces that exist between father and daughter and what familiar places become without their presence. Humourous and heartbreaking, these poems will stay with me a long time.' – Sabrina Mahfouz, author of *How You Might Know Me*

'These poems made me light a candle, find another blanket, crave fresh bread, and send thoughts to my loved ones many miles away.' – Jenna Clake, author of *Fortune Cookie*

'Gaia Holmes performs elegant feats, her language is effortless and remarkable.' – Helen Mort, author of *No Map Could Show Them*

'Holmes chronicles the stages of grief – the awareness of approaching death, the loss and the recovery – with searing lyricism. This emotional journey, with all of its turns, is met with adroit and luminous verse. Insightful and often witty, Holmes faces the trials of life not only with her deft elegiac touch but with reserves of humour.' – Poetry Book Society

## Acknowledgements

The author would like to thank Hawthornden Castle who awarded her a month's fellowship in 2017, enabling her to work on the poems in this collection. Thanks are also due to the following websites on which some of these poems appeared: *The High Window, 3 Drops from a Cauldron* and *Claudius Speaks*. 'Ballast' was commended in the Larkin Poetry Competition, 2013. 'Holes', 'Your Orange Raincoat', 'Kummerspeck' and 'Voyeur' were all commended in the York Mix Poetry Competition and the following poems were also commended in various poetry competitions: 'Kneading' (Ver Poets), 'And There was Just this Monstrous Hole' (Otley Word Feast). 'The Allure of Frost' first appeared in *The Butcher's Dog* magazine, 2015. 'I Belong Here' came third in the Carers UK creative writing competition in 2016 and appeared in print, alongside 'Hygge' in *Caring: Carers UK Members' Magazine* #44 in February 2017. 'Last Orders at the Light Bar' was awarded second prize in the Blackpool Wordpool Poetry Competition, 2014. 'Guests' won the Bare Fiction Prize 2016 in poetry.

## By the same author

*Dr James Graham's Celestial Bed*
*Lifting the Piano with One Hand*

First published in Great Britain in 2018 by Comma Press.
www.commapress.co.uk

ISBN: 1-910974-45-5
ISBN-13: 978-1-910974-45-2

Supported using public funding by
**ARTS COUNCIL
ENGLAND**

The publishers gratefully acknowledge assistance from the Arts Council England.

Printed and bound in Great Britain by Clays Ltd, Elcograf S.p.A.

# where the road
# runs out

GAIA HOLMES

# Contents

# And Still we Keep on Singing

Up here the hours go backwards
and we're closer to the edge of things.
Up here you have to know the language of the wind,
you have to understand the manners of mist and riptides
in order to go to sleep singing,
in order to wake up
on the brighter side of life.

Some days sunlight sugars the island.
Cats lie on their backs bleaching their bellies,
seals bask on the rocks, braise their lovely fat
until it's close to boiling point.
Orange crocosmia burns gently
around the mill dam.
Every kitchen smells of bread.
The world hums as it hangs out its washing.

Other days we gag on the reek of drift-tide rot.
Broken gulls and fulmars
float in the harbour
like oily rags.
Damp socks and dresses
freeze and stiffen on the washing line.
A furze of fret blots out our thin and precious light.
The glow of the mainland, that cosy grail we cling to,
that glimmer of cars, buses, shops and living,
disappears into the dark, monstrous mouth
of the island where lightbulbs shatter and fuses blow
and we're left with singed fingers, the thick stink of wax
and candles whose wicks are too damp and weak
to sustain a flame.

**Leaves**

There are worse things
than a loose tooth,
a ladder in your tights,
a burnt dinner.
There are worse things
than losing your keys.

My father is fevered
and godless.
My father is dying
on an island
with no trees.
I send him prayers.
I send him bulging sacks
of autumn leaves.

## I Belong Here

I belong here,
Mistress of Haar, Our Lady of the Seals,
your angel, your fumbling nurse, your little star,
stumbling around in your size 10 wellies
and your clay-crusted fleece,
stubbing my toes on shadows,
walking to the village shop
to buy red wine and Complan,
waving at the locals,
letting the mad winds bruise my cheeks
and twist my hair into witch-knots

I belong here
cooking stone soup every day,
beach combing for hope,
scrumping kelp and driftwood to burn
in our evening fires,
cooling your brow
with lavender on a mouldy flannel,
singing *love, love, love.*

I belong here
with the cracked windows,
the damp, your denial,
the wild and the raw,
the lying dog-eared books:
*How to Live to be 100,*
*How to Outsmart your Cancer,*
stacked between the jars of pills
and the sticky bottles of morphine
on your bedside table.

I belong here in December
with you and your three white cats,

grinding your tablets
to powder at midnight,
as the Orkney gales rock the caravan.

I belong here
with your dying
and every dawn sky
seething
and blistered
with stars.

**Feckless**

Sometimes it makes him angry, this dying,
and I keep doing things wrong,
forget to soften the stars with almond milk
before I bring them to his bedside on a saucer,
buy the wrong kind of green tea,
the wrong kind of holy water
from the village shop.

He says there are things that need darning
but I end up darning the wrong holes
so there is less light
and it's hard to read the instructions.

I have to sign lots of papers now
in order to be a proper daughter
and I keep writing my name backwards.
*Forgodsake,* he says, still strong enough
to make the caravan shake,
to make the clock fall off the wall,
to scare the fat white cats
from where they lay
scorching their fur on the gas fire.
*Forgodsake.*

And I know that I've lost
my angel's status
but I'm trying.
I've knackered my back
from trying to shift the moon,
angling it so it shines in to his room.
I've worn out my songs
from trying to teach the seabirds
to sing something sweet.
I've used up my prayers

from trying to persuade
the wind to lie down
and give us some peace.

He asks me if the miracles
he ordered from America
have arrived yet
and I have to tell him, no.
*Forgodsake.*
The island whimpers
and trembles beneath us.
There will be bruises
in the morning

and I keep doing things wrong,
rub bloodroot into his skin
deosil instead of widdershins
then drop the bottle,
burn sinkholes in the carpet.
*Forgodsake,* he says.

I sit at his bedside sucking my knuckles
until he slips in to fevered sleep
then I jog barefoot around the mill
in the frost to remind myself
that sometimes I need
to suffer.

## Hygge

Tonight, with you calm, clean,
smelling of lavender in your new pyjamas
and the fire I've been trying to kindle for hours
finally settling itself down to blaze
and crackle and glow,
I light all the candles I can find,
put Tallis on the stereo, sit holding your hand.

Tonight, the sea will be too wanton
to carry a ferry.
No one will come and no one will go
and in the morning there will be
no fresh bread or milk
on the shelves of the village shop.

Tonight we will keep the cats in.

Tonight, we will be landlocked and cosy
as rain pelts the windows like little pearls
and bolshy wind rocks the caravan.

Tonight I will feel your knots unravelling,
our bond thickening
as love and thin motets chase the cold
from the corners of the room,
and I will almost forget
that you are dying.

## The Wrong Kind of Birds

Morphine coaxes you away
from the practical things
on your mind –
the lawn you have to mow,
the bills you have to pay,
the will you have to write.
There is grass
creeping through the gravel
of your pristine drive,
duck shit bleaching
the path to the dam
but, for once,
you don't care.
'There are birds
singing in my head,' you say.
'Come closer so you can listen.'
and you grasp my hand,
clasp it hard so I can feel
the fevered tick
of your wayward pulse.
You pull me close
so that my ear
is pressed to your ear.
I hear nothing,
only the arid wheeze
that lives in your chest
and, outside,
the tactless cackle
of sea birds –
the ones with brutal names
and caws roughed-up
with oil-rig rust, fish scales
and drowning.
These, I think,

are the wrong kind of birds.
The birds in your head
must be sweeter –
the trilling, humming,
chirping kind,
the smooth inland
flower-eating kind
with pollen
in their feathers
and sap
in their throats.
I move away
but you pull me back.
'Keep listening,' you say,
'and you'll hear them
soon enough.'

## Stone Soup

Up here every night,
just for the hope
and the blessing
of something steaming
and bubbling on the hob,
I cook us stone soup.

The thin broth
tastes of the sea,
reminds you of how,
only weeks ago,
you'd scramble
over the shingle,
happy to bruise your shins
in the Bay of Balfour,
gulping down the briny air,
savouring its myth,
its tang, its babble.

Now you are bed-bound,
landlocked
so I tack a crumpled sea-view
from an old National Geographic
across your window,
bring the tide home
in old pickle jars,
pour grains of sand
into your cupped palms,
sing you to sleep
with hissing lullabies,
press crystals of salt
onto the tip of your tongue.

## The Lord's Prayer

This morning
the mist won't lift
to let the daylight in
and you are
definitely dying.
The rattling
behind your ribs
has stopped.
I hold a mirror
to your mouth
and your breath
makes no ghosts.

I have no manual
for dying
so I do what I think
you're supposed to do
in this situation.
I light the stub
of last night's candle,
utter something holy
and stand
at your bedside
with the unfamiliar taste
of the Lord's Prayer
clinging to my lips.

Definitely not dead,
you open your eyes
and say,
'What's that bloody rubbish
you're muttering?'

**Reek**

The days reek
of me – soused in Dettol,
kippered
by the miracle incense
I burn at his bedside,
and him – his body
going wrong.

Godless,
each night
I borrow faith.
Mumble clumsy Latin
as I douse the threshold
with Zoflora.

## Playing Alive

It's a kind of game they play,
him and the nurses
even though they all know
it's a matter of days.
They pretend he might be alright,
lay his freshly washed running socks
across his trainers on a chair
in case he feels like
taking a jog through the mizzle
down the hospital drive
in the middle of the night.
They hang his coat, ready to go,
on the back of the door.
They turn on the radio
for the weather
and the news at ten
and he pretends he still cares
about the density of rain
and the force of the wind,
about the world
beyond his body.
They read him the menu,
help him tick a box
then bring him soup
even though he cannot eat,
has not eaten for days.
He likes to inhale its flavours
as it steams in the shallow bowl
on his bed tray.
He likes to imagine
he is hungry and closer to life.
In sleep he gobbles down the air,
dreams of Lapsang Souchong tea
and mashed potato,

13

goes for a ten-mile run
across the tops of the waves
from the Kirkwall corn slip,
to the beach at Elwick Bay.

## The Weather

You're not used to this:
warmth on a dial,
double glazing,
this airless locked-in
sucked-in
almost-silence
punctuated
by the hum and tick
and bleep
of monitors, machinery
and the sticky
hush and kiss
of the nurses' shoes
in the corridor
outside your tepid room.

In here
nothing flutters.
Your unread papers sleep
still and deep
whilst December
mimes a storm
outside your window

and I want to bring
the weather in.
I want to let the wind
run around you
like a rabid dog.

I want the wild rain
to lash
your thin fevered limbs
and shock you
into living.

.s a dull, wet
liver-red light
that shines
from the dead tonight
and we have used up
all our candles.

Today, all day,
she has been
making things right,
telling the dust to leave,
polishing mirrors,
stewing the bed sheets
in sunshine,

and now, at dusk
I see the glow
of my mother
out in the garden
carrying naked flames
in her palms
like lotus buds,
warding off
the wolfish dreams,
the darkness,

and coaxing back
the good things
we have lost,
making them
cheese on toast
and cocoa
guiding them
to the lavendered

guest rooms
of our house,
saying, 'Dead or alive
you are welcome here.'

## Kummerspeck

Grief needs feeding.
At first we feed it sweet and boneless things:
memories, halva, meringue,
the songs the gone used to sing.
We feed it whole boxes of Cornish fudge,
marzipan gnawed from the block,
cold custard sucked straight from the carton

and for a while, we appease it
until it starts begging for blood
and then we turn to the dead things
and though we've not touched flesh for years
we find ourselves in the supermarket
filling our trolleys with meat –
the reddest, most visceral kind:
packs of mince and liver,
black pudding, knotty hearts,
plump kidneys, slabs of beef and livid steaks –
things that leak and mourn in colour
in their polystyrene trays

and though we cook without tears
our lonely kitchens smell of dying.
Our garish fridges
stink of butchers' gutters,
drift-tide rot, things on the turn,
gashes on the brink of gangrene.
Every meal's a little wound.
Our plates are holes
we cannot fill.
Like grief, our hunger
is edgeless.

**Preservation**

In spring
the dull iron footbridge
over the reservoir
starts to chirrup and sing,
greens and glitters
with a mass
of lusty, coupling toads.
For fear of crushing love,
she walks the long way home.

**Fixed**

They were rough and crusty with it.
Soap and water wouldn't wash it off.
It gritted the insides of their socks.
It smuggled itself beneath their fingernails
and flavoured everything they touched.
It inveigled its way into their words
so that everything they said
came out as a threat.

It trickled from their hair, their shoes,
their cuffs. They left crunchy trails of it
glittering in their wake.
They longed for bland and saltless days,
craved plain potatoes, unseasoned stews,
civil conversation.

They hallucinated it –
they were mummified, all their gaps
were pockets for it
or they were packed in it
like lemons or herring
or century eggs.

His ribs caged a salt mine.
Her heart was a salt lick.
They both tried to conquer it.
He scraped honey
from the neighbours' hives
and steeped his tongue in it.
She hid in the cupboard
under the stairs,
spooning sugar into her mouth,
practised being sweet.

They both dreamed of change,
imagined bananas
blackening in the bowl,
oranges blooming with mould.
But it fixed things.
It lived with them
and it wouldn't let things rot.

## The Hole Room

The whole room was filled with holes.
There were holes to put lost things in,
holes to put found things in.
There were holes to put holes of any size into.
There were also holes you could use to fill things,
holes that would slot into cheese or hosepipes,
donuts or B roads,
holes that would fill loneliness or hunger.

There were holes you could wear
like absence or Ascot hats,
holes like mousing cats,
holes that would catch and kill
every moving hole.

There were holes where
wholeness was kept behind glass
on velvet cushions
shining like Faberge eggs
or christening spoons
and these holes were the precious holes,
the holes you wouldn't want to fill
with anything else.

## In the Pancake Room

As we get older we become more pliant
and able to drape ourselves across the furniture,
lithe and giving as freshly tossed pancakes.
With our new skill there is no longer any need
for cushions and this is a good thing.
There is no need for curtains either.
We can just hang our doughy selves
from the curtain rail and keep the light out
for a while until we get bored of hanging around
and decide to have a go
at being a carpet.
Hopefully someday soon
you too will experience the joys
of laying calmly and beigely on the floor
expectantly waiting for a dollop of golden syrup
or something else as sweet
that will melt, without fuss,
into your warm, floury pores.

## Before All This

Before all this
there were phone calls,
there were letters,
there were postcards,
there were badly printed posters
in corner shop windows,
there were crowded notice boards,
there was proper conversation.
There were names and numbers
written in tipsy scrawl
on the peeled-off backs
of beermats.
There was ink.
There was paper.
There were crossings-out.

Before all this
we clung to the folklore of magpies
and sunsets.
We read the weather in seaweed
and common sense.
We all carried
umbrellas.
We did not know
how to edit our lives,
walked out raw into the world
every morning.
We placed our faith
in road maps
and sometimes
we got lost.
Sometimes
we found beauty
in the detour.

Sometimes
we were late.

Before all this
no one was really bothered
about what Jodie or Sandra or David
had for breakfast.
No one took photos of their dinner.
No one took photos of their bruises.
No one took photos
of the pulpy gore
the cat dragged in,
the rising damp,
the mouldy fruit,
the dead wasp on the window sill,
the traffic jam,
the stains on a Travelodge bedsheet.

Before all this
our smiles were never sepia or polaroid.
We had scars and gaps and cracks
and we were more honest.
We knew how to read
the language of the body.
We knew about patience,
the beauty of waiting.

Before all this
we had manners.
We looked.
We listened.
We never stroked our phones.

Before all this,
if we wanted to see
a blood moon, a harvest moon,

a shooting star,
we'd step outside.
We'd live in it.

Before all this
snow and autumn leaves
came without a hashtag.
We did not need an app
for relaxation or meditation.
We did not need an app
for empathy or humanity.
They were things we knew
how to do
without instruction
and we did them well.
We did good things
for the goodness
of doing them
and not for the ticks,
the gain, the glowing kudos.

Before all this
validation
was more than a click.
'Liking' came from our lips.
Love came with flesh.
Some parts of us were secret.
Some parts of us
were never shared.
Some parts of us
were never spoken.

## The Audition

She starts by giving him
her best smile
then flutters her eyelids
as if they're moths
trapped between the bulb
and the shade.

She recites the first 23 pages
of Joyce's *Ulysses*
to him backwards,
and in Russian,
whilst patting her head
and rubbing her belly
at the same time,
and mixing and shaking
a Long Island Iced Tea
with the other hand.

She pulls white rabbits
from her woollen cap,
balances on the table with her nose,
wraps her legs behind her neck
and wriggles her ears.

She wills Gladioli
to twist into bloom
from her lips,
tilts back her head,
turns her throat
into a vase,
opens the window
and blows out the lights
of the city
as if blowing out candles
on a birthday cake.

For her final trick
she takes a crowbar to her ribs,
cracks her heart
out of its cage,
and places it on the floor
where, like a clever circus bear,
it tap dances
to the rhythm of his pulse
before crawling up his body
and into his hands,
curling itself into a silky knot
and purring
like a hot, wet, new-born kitten.

And he looks at the blood,
he looks at the hole in her chest,
he looks out onto the un-lit night
and he says, 'No.'

**Google-it**

Encyclopaedias
all over the world
are seriously depressed.

Clean-cornered
and un-thumbed,
they are tying themselves
to railway tracks.
They are swallowing bleach
and carpet tacks.

They are forcing
the corners
of their dust jackets
into toasters
and jumping off bridges.

Hear them falling,
their spines cracking
with the friction,
their pages
shrieking.

See them falling
like flocks
of frenzied doves.

## Lack

He likes his parties best
when everybody's gone.
He walks around the house,
nibbles at their leavings –
their sandwich crusts,
the little half-moons of cake
that remain around
the crescent of their bites.
He lights up the fag-ends
from the ashtray in the porch,
riddles the cooling embers
of the fire they sat around
until they flare back into flame,
brushes up the mud of their lives
from where it hardens
on the welcome mat
behind the door.

He savours the fresh lack of them,
relishes their absence,
sips their sticky dregs of wine,
soaks up their spills,
bins their rinds and peels and pits,
presses his cold palms
against the warm clefts they've left
in the cushions on the chairs,
necks the last flat inches
in their bottles of beer
mulls over the richness
of the things they didn't say.

## Holes

As a child, his Grandfather told him
that the holes in Swiss cheese
were poisonous so, for years,
he ate around them.
He still has that fear.
Each night
as a woman leans across her lover
to turn off the lamp
or a man uses his wife's chest
as a pillow
or a mother lays her child
in its cot
and smooths down
its fuzz of new-born hair,
or a father sits
at his daughter's bedside
with a book and hot milk,
or an owl echoes back a hoot,
there's a hole in his house
which he nibbles his way around
neatly, like a mouse who has been
to finishing school.
His careful perforations
edge the rim of the chasm
like a collar of Chantilly lace,
distracting him
from the loneliness that gapes
in the middle of his bed.

## Kneading
*After Andrea Kowch*

Her life is full of gaps.
The barbed wire fell away
from their fences
leaving rotten posts.
Wind shucked the glass
from the greenhouse frame
and rabbits gnawed their apple trees
to stumps.

The turnips and beetroot they planted
are soft and rotten beneath the dirt
and the dry-teated cows
can give them nothing.

They sell what they can: rare eggs with no yolk,
scant scrapes of honey, the last plump fish
from their dying lake

and there's not enough love
in her wrists
to make bread.

In bed at night
her husband's hands
fall through her.

## Ballast

You reach a certain stage in your life
when you seem to spend a lot of time
holding other people's babies.

At parties, the bottles of M&S berry crushes
on the kitchen table
outnumber the bottles of wine
and it seems you're the only one drinking.

Tonight you're nursing your second glass of Chianti,
warming it against your chest
as the other guests sip mocktails
and talk of teething rings and Farley's Rusks
and you're trying to find a way in, but failing

and one of the kids is doing that cute thing again
with his hat pulled down to his nose
and everyone starts taking photos
and clucking and cooing and you take one too
just to fit in, even though you know
that you'll delete it later
in favour of a landscape
or something you can understand
or something you can have

and you want a cigarette but no one's smoking
so you go and stand outside the front door in the sleet
to smoke a roll-up but it gets wet
and you're sucking on nothing

so you go back in. You cut through the branny fug
of milk and nappies with your reek of smoke
and they look at you cow-eyed with pity
and you know they've been talking about you
and one of them says, 'It's not too late at forty'

and you mumble something and walk into the kitchen
to pour yourself another, bigger glass of wine
and you sit there for a while listening to them talking
and think about the things they have:
the husbands, the high chairs, the family-sized toasters,
the pairs of tiny red wellies lined up by the door,
the huge American fridges
covered with glitter-crusted playschool pictures
and you think about your lack.

You think about your cat that moved next door,
your scrawny basil plants withering on the windowsill,
the bread you bake always turning black

and you go back into the lounge,
move mounds of small, pale woollen things off a chair
and sit down wishing you had some ballast in your pockets,
wishing you were not made of straw and dry things,
wishing you were not quite so old and flammable
because they're all looking at you
and it seems you've turned into
the hollow witch levitating in the corner,
that lonely, awful thing
that they could have become.

## Angel of the Checkout
*After Anne Sexton*

Oh, Angel of the checkout,
do you know the price of love?
Does it have a barcode?
Can you scan it?
Can you weigh it like salmon
or a bag of lemons
or do you need to type
its numbers in?

Oh, Angel of the checkout,
do you know the price of love?
Is it raw? Do I need to cook it?
Can I feed it to my baby?
Can I feed it to my father?
Can I feed it to my cat?
Does it stain? Does it leak?
Does it burn? Does it come
with its own batteries?

Oh, Angel of the checkout,
do you know the price of love?
Is it machine-washable?
Do you stock the low-fat variety?
Do I keep it in a fruit bowl,
a bed or an ice box?
Do I need ID to buy it?
Do I need a licence for it?

Oh, Angel of the checkout,
do you know the price of love?
Have *you* tried it?
Did it make a difference?
Is it cheaper at Lidl?

Is it cheaper than longing?
Is it cheaper than hate?
If it doesn't work
can I bring it back?

## Your Orange Raincoat

Unlike the rest of the house,
which is softening under the lick of damp,
it remains, crackling and stiff,
hanging on the back of the cellar door –
your orange raincoat,
loud and kitsch as a Warhol tangerine.

Some days I stand there with my nose
pressed into the greasy creases of its cuffs,
snorting up engine oil and wood smoke,
remembering when things were really bad
and too much had died

and there was barbed wire between us in our bed
and each morning the cat left a mess of sparrow
on the doorstep
and our breakfast milk was always sour
and we could hardly talk to each other
and you said,
'Let's go up to the wind farm and scream,'
and I put on my flimsy brown kagool
and you put on your loud orange raincoat
and we drove up to the turbines in the rain

and the brusque air bashed our cheeks
and took our words
and we stopped trying to talk,
spread our arms, opened our mouths wide
and screamed

and it was better than trying to agree,
it was better than fresh milk,
it was better than sex.

## Those Spaces You Try to Fill

After midnight
and you're up with wine
and your quiet lamps,
carving yourself a little hour,
reminding yourself
of what you're not
in your notebook by the fire.

Isn't this what it might have been like,
for Plath, for Boland,
nudging the shadows away
as they spider the page.
This fat, safe moment of solitude
plumped out with snores
and sleeping babies
and neither nappies nor potatoes
boiling in a pot on the hob?

These women,
claiming the moonlight on the kitchen table
as their jackpot.
These women, trying not to bruise the air
with their elbows as they write,
trying not to wake the sleepers
with the clink of a glass, the scratch of a pen
or a gasp of light.

And it's sweeter, more charged
when done in secret,
when precious and hurried,
scrawled in the half-dark.
The words come thicker and rawer
when you think you might be
disturbed or discovered

hunched over your notebook by the fire
with a glass of wine and a quiet lamp
and moonlight pearling the kitchen table.

But your night has no edges,
no deadlines.
There are no small, hot fingers
creasing the silence.
So you invent a cry for the morning feed
and race against it.
Fill the lines with words
as your hollow body thickens
with milk.

## Milk
*After William Carlos Williams*

I wake up seething
in the middle of the night.
Afraid of setting the bed on fire,
I clamber over your sleeping body,
go to your kitchen,
open your fridge
and stand there cooling
in the peppery breath
of the ice box
as I drink all your milk.

Forgive me.
In the morning
there will be nothing
to pour on your cornflakes.

When I'm like this
the only things
that can soothe my ire
are acres and acres of snow,
the soft, pink belly of a dog,
the smell of the world
after rain,
a month of silence,
milk.

Forgive me.
Sometimes my filters
do not work.
Sometimes all the acid
inside me
gets into my veins
and comes out of my lips.

My words scorch the air
and burn on your back.
My kisses leave a rash
where I meant to leave love.
My good intentions
are charred.

This, alas,
is the curse of a woman
who burns quietly.

Where your fridge
is full of milk
and placid slabs
of cheese,
mine is full
of glowing coals
and forest fires
raging in old pickle jars.

## The Twitcher

That night the house moved again,
rocked an inch on its foundations
as if resettling itself
like a cat on a cushion.
This was the third time in a week
and each time it happened
the cups swayed a little
on their hooks in the kitchen,
the knives and forks
skittered towards the sink
from where they dried
on the draining board,
the soap plummeted off
the rim of the bath.
At first she thought
she was imagining it,
that perhaps the instability
was in her head
and began to worry about it,
the madness, the movement,
until someone told her
that most houses
moved from time to time.
It was quite normal,
and after that she had nightmares
about the house packing maps,
cheese and pickle sandwiches
and her best binoculars
and setting off at dawn
for an early morning ramble.
She imagined her and the children
rolling around its rooms
like loose beads,
cracking themselves

against the skirting boards
as it clambered over brooks
and leapt over ditches.
She imagined the light fittings
crashing against the ceiling
like wrecking balls
as it bounded excitedly
through the frost-crusted fields
on the trail of a small,
twittering, bluish bird
it had never seen before.

## The Mushroom Gatherer

We all wanted him to be our father –
this man with hands like shovels,
this man that could strike a flame
on a damp matchbox,
this man who could stave off the rain.

We all loved him
dangerously and quietly,
bit our knuckles in bed at night
when we thought about him
dusting the stars,
rolling the fat, dry moon into view.
Some of us prayed.

He smelled of burnt sky
and sawdust.
The grass was singed in his wake.
We all took photos of his footprints,
pressed them to our chests when we slept.

Each morning
I felt my poems
rotting in my throat
as I waited for him
to return from the woods,
his big fingers licked with dew,
his pockets full of mushrooms,
his words tasting of dirt.

There was something of God in his voice.
When he spoke,
my wild heart
lay down like a lamb
and blood lost its meaning.

My small words
stopped beating in my chest.

## Sacramental

You closed the curtains, pissed on the fire,
scraped a landscape off its canvas.
You took fuses out of plugs,
crow-barred the element out of its kettle,
poured good red wine down the drain.

You dialled his number
and left a gap on his phone.
He came and found you empty.
He shook you to bring the blood back
into your cheeks.
Your eyes and your teeth rattled in your head.
Your loose heart thudded against your ribs.
You laid across him like a sacramental wafer.
He said he could not feel you.
You asked him to pray for your mouth.

Whilst he was sleeping
you pricked his pulse into your arm
with the tip of a fish knife.
You filled his bag with stones
and brass dogs because you wanted him
to remember you when he left.
You wanted him to feel
the weight of you all day.

You took back your kisses,
laminated them
and sent them to your father,
set your screams in resin
and gave them to a museum.
You un-fattened the goose
and made it thin and free,
pushed the rain back into the clouds

and watched the slugs on the path
blett and wizen like medlars.

You wanted to murder someone
but instead you took a book
and cracked its spine.
You shaped his name
in bits of broken glass and ate it.
Your throat did not bleed.

## And There was Just this Monstrous Hole...

When she saw the sinkhole on the news
she started inching closer to the edge of things,
moved the furniture against the walls,
would not walk across the middle of the room.
The TV footage showed a raw-eyed man
standing beside the gape that ate his brother.
The camera zoomed in on the chasm.
It was dark except for a scrap of tartan shirt
clinging just below the rim, fluttering
in the breeze of the maw like party bunting.
She imagined it reeked, belched out a stink
like boiled turnip and woodland truffles.
The bereft man explained how his brother
had sat down to eat his Sunday lunch,
was just salt-and-peppering his mash
when the kitchen floor opened up
and took him and the table. After that
she couldn't get the image out of her head,
the horrible minute when it sucked them in,
him and the table, followed by marrowfat peas
and swathes of gravy. She couldn't stop thinking
about all those sinkholes moling away
in the ground beneath her feet,
trying to decide where to open themselves,
which bit of someone's life to swallow –
their car, their horse, their hedge, their husband.
She thought about setting huge traps for them
with savage jaws and springs and iron teeth,
traps powerful enough to catch and kill
their nothingness.

## Reporting Back

More with me dead
than when he was alive,
my father is everywhere.
I see him
levitating above the fountain
in People's Park
or making chapattis
with spelt flour and star dust
over a campfire
on the side of the road.

He pops round in his spare time
to bring me something celestial
to put in one of my poems –
an angel's feather in a Jiffy bag,
a clutch of notes plucked from a lyre,
a zephyr in a Marmite jar.
And sometimes he stays for a while,
sits in a corner of the room
muttering at the news
or writing lists of things to do
as I get on with my life.

He's still not much of a conversationalist.
I want to know how it is to be dead.
I want to know how it is 'up there.'
I ask him about the people, the landscape,
the weather and he sighs,
adds a word to his list, says:
'Well, I'll tell you this much.
They do good chips in heaven.'

## 1 Afterwards

we keep losing our balance,
reach out
to steady ourselves
on walls or songs
or words
that are no longer there
and we fall.

The bruises darken
on the inside.
We feel them blooming
under our skin.
We say nothing
but they ache in us
all day,
hum their sad tunes
through our veins.

And though
the pain leaves
when we go to bed
we're kept awake
by the sound
of bones
too small to name
breaking
in our bodies.

## Driving

I'm driving up the A9 –
one hand on the wheel,
the other
holding my heart in
as we slalom
through spring rabbits,
skidding on blood,
crunching over skulls.
It's an awful feeling,
this sacrifice,
this lack of control.
It's an awful sound,
these little deaths
we keep making.
*Haven't we done*
*enough already?*
I ask you,
wanting to pull over,
light incense
and sing something
loud and holy
from the lay-by
but you turn to me
with a look that could
flatten the Cairngorms,
tell me *This is all*
*part of life,*
*this driving*
*through the pain,*
tell me to keep driving,
and, wanting to stay
on your good side,
I do.

## Remembering Light

*The San José mine, Chile, August 2010.*

### 1. Pulse

We are deep, deep down,
deeper than the dark,
deeper than the dead.

We do not know
that, up above,
they have not forgotten us.

We do not know
that they are not yet
looking for relics
to cling to,
scouting our houses
for strands of our hair,
the last cups we drank from,
the ghosts of our sweat.

We do not know
that they are not yet
lighting candles
on our shrines,
screwing down the lids
on our empty coffins.

We do not know
that, up there,
they can hear us weeping.
They press their palms
against the mountain
like stethoscopes
and feel our small hearts
pulsing through the diorite.

## 2. Forgotten Things

When you're so deep down
you are closer to the things
you hoped you had forgotten.
We hear them rustling against the rock
like bone-hungry rats.
We hear them scurrying and hissing:
our lies, our anger, our greed,
everything we have broken: limbs,
cups, clocks, hearts, plates
and promises.
We see their red eyes glowing
through the pitch
reminding us
of our cracked but beautiful lives.

## 3. Bedlam

Two weeks in the deeps, in the darker-than-the-dead, in the
devil's pitch-black pocket, we are losing it. Our bones are
sticking out. We rub our clavicles until our fingers bleed. We
rock on our haunches. We swear. We cry. We spit. We bark. We
bite. We try to gnaw our way through the endless night. We
blaspheme the ungodly dark. We lick the rocks, our tongues
hunting for threads of water, stains of light in every crack.
Some of us scream inwards. Some of us scream outwards. We
are greasy moles in the belly of Bedlam head-butting the walls,
begging the darkness to soften and sing us lullabies: *Sing for us
now in our hour of need. Sing us out of this hole. Sing us bright,
clear-eyed and upright.*

## 4. Naming Saints

Even the godless amongst us
are praying.
Even the godless amongst us
know the names of saints
when we need them.
And, God, we need them now.
We need their light to reach us
like the impossibility
of milk poured through tar.

In the dark we make a chain,
saints slipping off our tongues,
filling the edgeless hours
with holy notions:
St Lucy, with her salver full of eyes.
St Barbara, taming the lightning.
St Christopher. St Raphael. St Anne.
St Ambrose. St Columban.

The saints do not mind
our raw, guttering eyes,
our filth, our clammy vernacular.
The faithful lend the faithless
their thumb-buffed rosaries.
We click through the heavy minutes.

We hope.
We pray.


## 5. Things that Sparkle

And when we've used up all our saints, we look for things that
sparkle, shine and glitter in the beams of our headlamps down

in this dingy maw: miniscule freckles of ore in the rock, the
white of our teeth, the whites of our eyes, our sweat, the gloss
of thick saliva on our thirsty lips, buttons, buckles, watch faces,
the lenses of our glasses, the oily lustre on our hair, the taut and
shiny skin over our scars, the tarnished crucifixes around our
necks, our wedding rings.


## 6. Remembering Light

And when we've catalogued everything
that sparkles, shines and glitters
in the beams of our headlamps
down in this dingy maw
we have to remember the light
from above, and when we remember it
our eyes turn into shot-glasses.
We knock it back, we neck it,
we down it in one: the coppery lustre
of the city pavements after rain,
knives and forks draining by the kitchen sink,
the flare of a match,
the glowing tip of a Marlboro,
sunlight singing black shine
on the feathers of a scavenging crow,
the glow of July blessing lemons in the fruit bowl,
moonlight dozing on the pillows
beside our sleeping wives and children
and every loyal, reliable dawn
that seeps through the dark
to make a new morning.

We knock it back, we neck it,
we down it in one –
the memory of light.

## 7. Edges

we have lost our outlines
we do not know where our bodies
end we share the same aches
and our names are a tangled mess
our nightmares leak
into each other's ears
we drink the thin inches
from the same scabby cup
we have cast aside
the names of days
we no longer need them

we are trying to reinvent the night
because down here
in the grabbing roots of the mountain
there are no edges everything
overlaps everything coagulates
into one impenetrable clot

we scratch a line in the dust
and call it 'dawn'.


## 8. Desert Blooms

As we lie in the pit
on our cardboard mats
deep, deep, down,
deeper than the dark,
deeper than the dead,
sweating and stewing
in the foetid geothermal guts
of the mountain,
we like to imagine

that, up there, it is raining,
cold, fast, heavy rain.

We like to imagine
those dormant corms
and desert seeds
licked into life
by the deluge,

and in our fevered dreams
we joy-ride the tips of their shoots,
we climb them, cling to them
as they sear through the desert's crust
and we are freed by every flaring bud.
We are the añañuca, the chuparosa,
the bright doquilla unfolding,
you might hear us singing
as we open.
You might hear our petals
crooning in the feisty light.

## In Passing

We might have passed each other
at Gretna Green
as you headed South
and I headed North
up through Kingussie, Aviemore
and Invergordon
to where the road runs out
at Dunnet Head.

We might have passed each other
on the skinny road through Biggar
you, counting roadkill
and clocking the miles,
me, shedding my clothes
in the passenger seat,
high on the promise of brack and brine,
stitching my self back in
to my selkie skin.

## Stay Misty for Me

Something soft
has tickled him awake
into a morning
coddled with mist.

The snarling rocks
of Blackstone edge
are gentled with it.
The bony spines
of the hills
are cushioned.

He wants a coat
purled
with its shifting yarns.

He wants to fill an aquarium with it
and put it at the end of his bed.

He wants to melt into it.

What wakes her
is the feeling
that she's wrapped
in damp cling film.

When she looks
out of the window
what she sees is mist
choking the moorland
like an ether-soaked rag.

What she sees
is mist so thick

you could bury a body in it,
mist so thick
it could strangle your name.

She wants to take out
an injunction
against it.

She wants to gag
the letterbox
and seal all the cracks
in the house
with Gaffer tape
to stop it getting in.

## Someone to Blame

Convenient, as always, to have someone to blame
for the downfall of trees, the downfall of mankind,
the weather.

Emma, Katrina, Irma, Eve.
You can smell us coming,
There's a hint of the Arctic on our frosty breath,
worm-riddled apples rotting in our pockets.
We arrive, our sequined clutch bags
bulging with rolls of black ice,
power cuts and frozen pipes.

They say behind our frigid smiles,
we're horny as hell.
They say we sleep with snakes and cyclones
and when we start knitting, they worry
as they hear the mean clack-clack
of our needles, our bloody fingers
purling plagues and hurricanes,
our sweet mouths hatching Armageddon.

We're out when no one else is,
standing on the highest hills
smothering the valleys
with our colossal sacks of snow,
mashing tulips and daffodils,
cranking up the wind,
etching the windows with frost,
pushing the world deep, deep down
below zero.

## What Pylons Dream of

Pylons dream of
power cuts.
They dream of
shedding their danger
and stepping into ball gowns,
ivy and sheer stockings.
They dream of stitching
wads of flesh
onto their iron ribs
filling their frames
with little bones.
They dream of owning
hearts and sweat.
They dream of fat
and motion,
warm slow blood
thickening their wires.

Pylons dream of
pegging out the washing,
doing crosswords,
tickling kittens,
winding babies.

They dream of cycling back
from the village shop
with baskets full of bread and milk
hooked onto the handlebars
of their creaking bikes.

They dream of passion and static,
of plunging fingers into heather,
finding a pulse in the hummocks
singing it back to the sky

and sniffing
their muck-scented knuckles.

And some pylons dream
of toppling into the sea.
Some pylons
imagine the fizzing rip tides
they'll create
as they fall into the water,
the way they'll make
the ocean boil,
the mushroom clouds
of shocked fish
and savaged coral
that will bloom
in their wake.

## The Allure of Frost

Boxing day.
No fire in the grate and unopened presents
stacked around the base of the tree and fairy lights muted,
switched off, and the brandy that swells the fruit starting to eat
the cake in its tin and all the mirrors doused with tea towels
and your raw-eyed mother keening into a pillow in her
bedroom
and too many men in black whispering and nodding
and I don't know what the rosary is and whether to curtsey
to the priests when I hand them their tea
and the phrase 'fruits of thy womb' seems too ripe and too rich
for this and, Mary Mother of God, I don't know
how to cross myself and fear I'm invoking the devil
and the scent of death's so thick
that it's tainted the water and it's heavy in the curtains
making them bend the rail
and your lips taste of the oils that grease your dead sister
and when I kiss you, you push me away and I want to spit
and weep and slap the corpse where she lies in her coffin
all done up with hair grips and lipstick,
her sunken cheeks plumped out with wads of cotton wool
and the rictus of sin softened
by the crust of Rimmel Natural Beige powdering her face
and it's so hot in here
that the cheese is sweating and the butter is liquid.
The chocolate coins are dripping from the tree.
Your Aunt's un-bitten sandwiches
are curling upwards on her plate
and the lilies are wilting and stinking in their vases
and the cat stands quivering and retching
against the cold crack beneath the back door.
Outside the frost, not knowing any different,
continues to sparkle. And I'd like to go out there.
I'd like to stand in it until my feet turn blue.

## Voyeur

The doctors
and solicitors of suburbia
are waking.
Barefoot and rosy
they glide around their houses
in sheer satin nighties
and thin pyjamas.

Up here, packed in layers
of socks and fleeces,
my knuckles are blue
and my rooms are cold.
Frost patterns my duvet.
Ice glosses the spines
of my books
and my porridge
never boils.

Chilly voyeur, I squint
into their central-heated lives,
try to scrump some warmth
from those easy places
where butter melts into bagels,
honey oozes off cosy spoons,
Granola grains puff and swell
in tepid bowls
and milk does not freeze
around the Special K.

Even with good binoculars
I can't see their breath.
I can't see their feet touching the floor
as they float around their balmy kitchens.
I can't tell if they're human.

**Thermals**

He always kept things warm for me –
the front door, the bed, the teapot.
He had these thermal fingers
he'd press onto things,
a kind of laying-on-of-hands
that could defrost a frozen chicken.

Once, when there was a power cut,
we made toast on his palms
and even managed to boil up
a small camping kettle to make tea.

When he was around
frost wouldn't settle on the window panes.
Cats curled around his legs
as if they were stove pipes.

When he was around
our breath was invisible.
The air had no angles.
He nudged the whole, cold world
to the liquid edge of melting
but if I wanted ice
he gave me ice.

## The Great Storm of '53

And afterwards
the world is calm.
Some gentle god
must have smoothed the sea
with his palms.

You could hardly tell
that last night a storm
turned the island inside out
apart from a few bald barns,
fences flattened
against the ravished grass,
fields rucked up
like slept-in beds

and down on the beach
broken eggs and scarlet claws
poking through the flotsam,
hundreds of flame-coloured cockerels
and stiff ginger hens
tangled up with the shucked mussels
in the wet, black seaweed
along the strand-line.

## Trip Switch

It was the middle
of a month of summer storms.
Broad beans mushed
and blackened in their pods
before they ripened.
Fat slugs the size of mice
gnawed the world back to the stalk,
glossed my nights with patterns of slime,
and you turned up dripping at my door
wearing petrichor like cologne.

The house tried to warn me.
Something popped, sparked
and charred in the fuse box.
The lamp spat out the flimsy glass of its bulb
and you took over.
Light hummed on the tips of your teeth.
Moths flocked at the edges of your smile
and I too, wanted to tap your light.

When I awoke in the morning you'd gone.
Instead of a note, you'd left your outline
scorched into the bed sheets.
I imagined you leaving the house,
you – posting my hot key
back through the letter box,
you – sizzling as the morning mist
licked your skin.
I imagined you crackling
as you walked down my street
melting the hearts of women, stones,
dogs and men
burning yourself away from me.

## Last Orders at the Light Bar

The cheapest you can buy is the thick, bruised light
that follows heavy rain,
the brash blue glare of fly-repellent lights,
the mean frowzy light from high-rise stairwells
or the soft, speckled gold of a microwave
cooking its load in the darkness.

Middle of the range is the subtle kind:
light glossing a bowl of green apples,
the muted glimmer of Koi carp in a pond,
sea light squeezed and filtered through a porthole,
the amber Rembrandt bloom of a country pub at night
or the quick flash of first light
bouncing off cans of Strongbow in the corner shop.

The pricey one that's craved but rarely drunk
is the afterglow.
They say it's like drinking silk or blended glow-worms.
Those who've drunk it wear its warmth for weeks.
At night their fingertips crackle like bonfire sparklers.
Their tongues are embers in their mouths.
The insides of their throats are the colour of foxfire.

Some get hooked, drink too much
and acquire an insincere dazzle.
Light thickens on their teeth,
their smiles become punches.
Everything pales beneath their touch
and their bodies bleach the bed sheets.

## Shadow Play

He came in winter
when the house was always dark,
brought red Christmas cacti
fire-crackering from their pots
and a suitcase full of candles,
thickened my gloomy rooms
with light.

I met the shadows he bred
without caution
and did not complain
when he followed me to my bed.

Outside, frost had edged the world
with spite.
The city foxes were howling,
cracking their teeth on the ice.
The sharp scent of January scared me.
His big hands cast wolves on the walls.
Fear made me knot myself
around him.

He had a bristled chin
and smelled of fathers.
'Tell me a story,' I said
and he told me how lust
could turn an angel
inside out.

## The Day the Sky Turned Black
*On reading the headline 'Crows cause blackouts in Japan.'*

You smell it first – the oily sheen on feathers,
wormy beaks, the whiff of old meat
and pizza crusts

and then the bland day bruises,
fills with wing and raucous *caw*
and the fluttering clot grows,
blocks out the sun,
mutes the promise of the moon.

The skyline sighs, preparing itself
for the black weight of birds.

Some of us are frightened,
lock all our doors and windows,
bubble-wrap our houses
and run down to our cellars
with crates of water
and tins of peaches,

but some of us do not worry,
knowing that crows know things
we do not know.

Some of us lean out into the squalor
of this fake city night
hungry for the message,
the knowledge,
the deep-throated, savoury words.

## The Runners Versus the Ramblers

We're rambling up the slope of Warley Moor
when we start to hear the rumbling
and they come, sweat-licked and glittering,
over the horizon.

Sun flashes off their number plates,
their water bottles, their lycra-clad thighs
as they thunder towards us like juggernauts,
mashing frogs and bees,
flattening the heather.

'Get out of the way! Runners coming!'
one roars and we're nudged off the path
and into the bog.

Their legs shine with wet mud
and bilberry gore,
they've swallowed marshes
with their running shoes
and they hiss or glare at us
for being so slow,
for being so dry-footed,
for being so pain-free and easy.

Number 252 is wearing a t-shirt
that says 'Grin and bear it!'
but she's not grinning.
Number 126, a frail looking runner
with knobbly knees
and a red sweat-soaked bandana
tied around his head,
snarls 'MOVE!' and shoves me
into a ditch with the heel of his hand.

They get more vicious.
Number 133 pulls a Beretta
from the waistband of her shorts
and waves it at us
as she leaps across a tussock.
Number 97 is carrying
a shrieking grouse in his mouth.
Its blood and feathers beard his chin.
Its dying heart pulses on his tongue.

And they keep coming,
pummelling the peat and sphagnum,
fisting the air,
spraying sweat like wet dogs,
scowling and glaring,
muttering and swearing,
until the last one
has passed us by
and the thunder stops
and the sore ground
is raw and steaming.

The bruised moorland quivers and moans,
tries to resurrect its crippled ling
and deer grass,
tries to plump out
its crushed frogs and bees
with the kiss of life.

## Road Salt

Snow falls fatly, prettily,
whites out the dog-eared leavings
of Christmas,
dolls-up the ragged end of January,
mutes the road between us
with its whispering glamour
and we're stuck –
you in the East and me in the West
with miles too thick and deep to cross

and, once again,
without you, I fall asleep
listening to the frost
patterning the insides of my windows,
lacquering the edges of my bed.

If I could
I would send you
seal-skin boots and brandy.
I would send a sledge
and a savvy husky to guide you
across the blinded miles,

but instead I go out
into the bright, dumb darkness
with my pockets full of road salt,
toss it to the night
like chicken feed,
try to melt myself
a path to you.

## Rain Charm for Stirling Street

Oh, the itch and nag of it –
this rainless month
when sapless slugs
fruit our yards like prunes
and the lawns
in the salubrious parts of town
are brown whispers.

Even inside
red roses yellow
and spill their petals
before they've had time to bloom.
Hard green mangoes
rot before they've ripened
and in the fridge
milk thickens and clots
in the necks of bottles,
the cheese gets louder and louder
until it roars.

And lately, we have had
restless nights too hot to touch,
deserts between us in our beds,
Sirocco winds blistering our dreams,
our waking bodies
black with fruit flies.

All you sun-junkies,
you lovers of deck chairs
and Ambre Solaire, forgive me.
I am taking action.
I am standing behind the kitchen door
wobbling a crosscut saw
to make the sound of thunder.

I am cooking lightning
in the microwave.
I am pouring rice onto a saucer
to make the sound of rain.
I am summoning a storm.

**Your Fault**

They blame it on me, say I must have stirred my tea
the wrong way, kneaded my dough without love,
dropped a stitch, burnt the bacon, lost the plot.

See me in the tabloids, photo-shopped:
my hair, a hurricane, my lips glistering with frost,
my cold smile cracking, and behind me
my odd-socked children buttoned-up all wrong,
branches breaking, cars skidding on black ice
and crashing into walls, things bruising in my trail.

They say, *It's your fault, your fault.*
*You must have left the door open*
*that night you were necking gin.*
*You must have let it out.*
*You should have caged it,*
*tied it up, trained it with a muzzle,*
*wired its jaws shut so it couldn't*
*rag the skyline, sink its teeth into the hills*
*and pop them out of their skins,*
*drag the fleecy stuffing*
*out of the land.*

They have sent the police out. They have sent out soldiers
with trucks full of road salt, cordon tape and anti-freeze.
The blue-fingered council are gritting the streets.
They have put a red warning next to my name.
My mad, cruel face flashes on every screen.
*Your fault. Your fault,* I hear them say
as I watch the black storm chasing its tail,
foaming and snarling outside my window,
growling at the frightened winter sun,
barking down the snow.

## Bloom

6 a.m. and in People's Park
the women bloom through the mist
to run their morning laps
before toast has been buttered,
before paratha and chapatti dough
has been kneaded and set aside,
before wet clothes have been pegged
from the line in the yard.

Some run in dazzling white trainers,
some in jewelled flip-flops that kiss out
flimsy percussion on the tarmac paths.
And how alive and free they seem —
these women,
as they streak, dawn comets of silk,
their scarves trailing behind them,
spreading the bright word
of saffron and purple,
their colours singing as they shimmer
past the pale statues of Greek gods,
the formal flower beds,
the pond full of coke cans
and mangy ducks
the peeling sun-bleached benches
where no one ever sits.

## Imported Goods

When she moved onto the street
she brought a wilderness with her.
After van loads of sofas, fridges,
standard lamps and bed frames
came pots of oak, sycamore,
wild garlic and bluebells.
She brought a tea-chest full of rooks,
an Ali Baba basket full of rabbits,
a shoebox full of voles and dormice
and a little stream,
patterned with streaks of minnow,
that she rolled out on the pavement
like a Turkish rug.

After a month her terraced house
was thatched with a mesh
of honeysuckle and ivy,
birds were building nests
and laying eggs in her guttering,
emerald moss had cladded
her drainpipes
and a small woodland had grown
in her six-foot yard.

Generally
the other residents of the street
were sweetened
by the sight of butterflies
brightening the tired beige washing lines,
kingfishers flashing on the dustbins,
skulks of foxes
glowing outside the corner shop
or forget-me-nots
growing through the concrete

but for some who were used to
nothing but the early morning roar
of traffic on the flyover,
the babble of the street
and the fat dawn chorus
were too much
and they complained about the noise
to the council.

## The Morning we Dragged the Settee into the Garden

it was a morning
when you were still a guest in my bed,
when you were still
testing out my name on your tongue
like 'laverbread', like 'sushi',
like something you'd never tasted.

It was a morning
when the last cold rind of winter
was giving in to spring
and I wanted to be with you
and out in it.

I wanted to douse my wrists
in its pollens.
I wanted to roll in the grass
and soak up the new season
like a dog rolling in dung.

## The Midge Hour

It's the blue hour, the midge hour, in Orkney
and the swallows are going mental –
swooping and scribbling the sky
as I peel red potatoes
over the kitchen sink.

I am trying not to think
about the man fishing in the harbour,
his writhing sack full of half-dead mackerel
spilling out, screaming dying silver
in the weak September light.

I am trying to forget
the greedy shriek of hungry gulls,
the wet slap-slap-slapping of death
on the cold concrete by the creels.

I am wondering
how some hands can club a herring,
break a chicken's neck,
or drown a pillow case of kittens,
without remembering love.

### How to Please the Sea

Tell it you like it best
when it's wild,
angry blue-black
and boiling,
throwing scallop shells
like plates
at a Greek wedding.

Tell it you are drawn
to its dark side –
its deep briny pockets
harbouring shipwrecks
and stingrays
and things that stun.

Tell it you like it
better than land,
*much, much better,*
so unpredictable,
*so, so clever,*
with its neap tides,
its riptides,
its masses
of rosy brain coral.

Give it your secrets
sealed in bottles,
scratched into its sands,
wept into rock pools,
stitched into kelp
and bladderwrack.

Tell it its lusty lick
has left a rash on your ankles

that you never want to lose,
that you will hide
beneath your inland socks
like a love bite.

## Being a Seahorse

I lie on your living room floor
changing colour in the weak December light,
wind-milling my arms as fast as I can,
making the dust rise like smoke
from your Turkish rug.

If I was at home my mother
would tell me to stop it,
she'd say 'You don't look as graceful
as you think you do.'
My dad would say 'If you have to do that,
please do it outside,'
and the cat would turn its back on me.

You, however, seem to like it,
move the furniture out of the way
so I can do my 'fast fin' stuff
unhindered,
say 'Wow!' each time I cling
to the leg of the coffee table
and change colour.

I tell you I've got a strong craving
for brine shrimp.
You say you'll do your best,
go out and return
with three tubs of M&S prawn cocktail.
'Lovely,' I say, 'Thank you,
that's just lovely.'
'Wow!' you say and sigh
as I show my gratitude
by turning a deep, rich shade
of Prussian Blue.

## Wild Pigeons
*After Mary Oliver*

You do not have to love me.
You do not have to walk through blizzards
to buy me Ibuprofen.
You only have to hold me
and pretend you mean it.

Tell me about your ex
and I will tell you about mine
as we eat Doritos,
down Chianti like Ribena
and feel the salt and the lack
burning on our lips.

Meanwhile, life goes on.
The street-lads' park
outside my house
to smoke skunk,
neck Red Bull
and listen to gangster rap
as they always do.

Meanwhile,
the mangy pigeons
flap and coo beneath the flyover
as the old Pakistani man
feeds them stale chapattis,
his white tunic
and voluminous trousers
fluttering in the back-draft
of the rush hour traffic
like prayer flags.

## The World's Sharpest Knife

When the days begin to shrink
we bank up the fire,
stopper the keyholes
with chestnuts and acorns,
wrap ourselves in bear skin
and go to bed early
with the last streaks
of dusk
still glowing on our lips.

In sleep our limbs knot,
our bodies lock.
Your heart borrows my beat.
My weak lungs
borrow your breathing.
Your fingers end
where mine begin.
When you turn, I turn
and we are so tightly woven
that the world's sharpest knife
couldn't cut us apart.

# Hope

Though it seems so dark
and the ceiling of the world's a wound
and so many hours have been bruised,
and so many lives have been broken,
there are stars up there tonight
and we must name them,
we must love them,
we must whistle them down like dogs
in faith of their shine
and they will be loyal.
They will show us where their bones are.
They will teach us
their soft, bright tricks of devotion.

And even on the blackest nights,
when hope and protest
are knotted in our throats,
when our smiles have been tarred
and buckled with the weight and stain
of shadows,
we have to remember they are there,
those glittering sky-hooked prayers,
prickling and humming,
embedded in that thick and lovely blue,
guarding us from spite,
keeping the moon from slipping,
herding the pale lamb-like dawns
into our sleeping houses
where they flow
through all our rooms
fluent and loving as milk.

# Notes

### I Belong Here
*Haar* (n): in meteorology, a cold sea fog, usually occurring on the east coast of England or Scotland between April and September.

### Hygge
*Hygge* (n): a Danish word which, roughly translated, means, the art of building sanctuary and community, of inviting closeness and paying attention to what makes us feel open hearted and alive. To create well-being, connection and warmth. A feeling of belonging to the moment and to each other.

### Kummerspeck
*Kummerspeck* (n): a German word used to describe the excess weight gained from emotional overeating. Literally translated, it means 'grief bacon'.

### Remembering Light
The San José mine in the Atacama Desert, Chile, is a mine from which gold, copper and iron were extracted. In August 2010, the mine collapsed trapping 33 miners. It was 69 days before they were rescued.

### Desert Blooms
After rare and intense rain falls in the north of Chile, parts of the usually arid Atacama Desert turn into a carpet of flowers. The 'desierto florido' (flowering desert) phenomenon usually occurs every five to seven years when rains cause buried seeds to germinate and flower.

### Someone to Blame
During World War II, American meteorologists started giving tropical storms women's names – often the names of their

wives and girlfriends – to help clarify weather information for pilots. In 1953, the American National Weather Service adopted the practice. In 1979, after critics pointed out that the practice of using only female names was at best unkind, things changed. Today, lists of alternating masculine and feminine names are put in a six-year rotation.

### The Great Storm of '53

In January 1953, Orkney was battered by one of the worst storms in the islands' recorded history. Although some 2,300 people perished across Britain and the Netherlands during the so-called 'great storm', miraculously, no one was killed in Orkney. However, the population of hens in Orkney was not so lucky. Henhouses were overturned and smashed to splinters, and in some cases blown out to sea. Dead birds were strewn everywhere. In Rousay, they were scooped up by the barrowload.

Fisherman recalled hearing the squawking of hens under the cover of a henhouse floating out to sea. According to them, the birds lived, for a time at least, in the sanctuary of an air bubble. – From www.orkneyjar.com

### Last Orders at the Light Bar

Inspired by a typo on a menu which offered 'deep fried lamp' instead of 'deep fried lamb'.

### Being a Seahorse

Seahorses propel themselves by rotating their fins approximately 35 times per second. During the courting ritual their bodies change colour.